Katie Piper

Confidence

THE JOURNAL

Quercus

Introduction

We'd all like to be a bit more confident, to have the courage to move outside our comfort zone and stretch ourselves, to reach our potential and to lead a satisfying and successful life. But I know that sometimes it is hard to know where to start. How can we grab onto more of this elusive thing called confidence? What is it that is holding us back?

These are all questions I've asked myself over the years. I realised that confidence is something we find within ourselves. We are in charge of digging deep within ourselves and releasing that inner confidence that is lurking there somewhere, I promise.

And so the idea for *Confidence: The Journal* was born. Every day you will take a new step towards achieving greater courage and self-esteem, without making daunting, drastic changes. This is something that will aid you on your own very personal journey, with tips, exercises and affirmations for every day of the year. With space to chart your thoughts and progress, this journal will help you achieve the level of confidence, success and happiness that everybody deserves.

Good luck on your confidence journey!

Love

Katie Piper

January

1 JANUARY

The new year is the perfect time to make a fresh start and there's no better way to start it than with a wish list. Write down all the things you would like to achieve in the year ahead:

....

....

....

....

....

....

....

....

....

....

....

2 JANUARY

This is the beginning of anything you want. Make some wishes and believe they can come true.

3 JANUARY

Focus on the good things in life, no matter how small, and they will multiply.

4 JANUARY

Ditch the negative inner commentary and replace it with positive thoughts. Instead of 'I'm hopeless at making new friends' how about 'My close friends rely on me and we make each other laugh'?

Jot down some positive thoughts here:

....
....
....
....
....
....
....
....
....
....

5 JANUARY

Confidence isn't about being perfect, it's about being
a worthwhile person.

6 JANUARY

Appreciate your body and what it does for you. Go for a walk – it
doesn't matter where to! You'll feel invigorated and refreshed.

7 JANUARY

Stop judging yourself and others. Focus on positive inner
messages and give yourself and others a chance.

8 JANUARY

Make the most of what you've got rather than
wishing you were different.

9 JANUARY

What is confidence? How would you define it? Stop and
think about what the word means to you.

10 JANUARY

Put a little bit of 'me' time into each day and use it to do
something you enjoy. Over the next few days, make a note of
at least three things you do each day that bring you joy.

....

....

11 JANUARY

....

....

....

12 JANUARY

....

....

....

13 JANUARY

High self-esteem comes from within and has to
be a conscious choice.

---

14 JANUARY

Listen to your own needs and desires and have the
confidence to say **no** when you need to.

15 JANUARY

It can be hard to find the time to keep up with friends.
Make today the day you call a friend who you haven't spoken
to in a while, or even send them a card. You'll make their day
and you'll feel good for it too.

16 JANUARY

Laugh! Tell a joke, or listen to one, share a funny story
or do something that you know will make you laugh.
Instant happiness boost!

17 JANUARY

How self-aware are you? The better you get to know yourself,
your strengths and your weaknesses, the easier it is to make the
right choices for you.

18 JANUARY

Appreciate three things about yourself. Your looks, your health, a particular ability, something good you did today, someone you helped? There's a long list of possibilities. Write them down and come back to them whenever you need a confidence-boosting pick-me-up.

1.

2.

3.

19 JANUARY

Are you stuck in bad habits that are holding you back?

Choose one bad habit that you'd like to ditch this year
and write it down.

20 JANUARY

Cook a healthy meal today and share it with someone you love.

21 JANUARY

Take a long, pampering bath or shower.

22 JANUARY

Positive change can begin whenever you wish it to.
Just embrace it.

23 JANUARY

Smile at someone in the street today. You will be surprised by
how much it lifts your spirits and theirs.

24 JANUARY

You have an inner strength that might surprise you. It is there,
waiting to be discovered.

25 JANUARY

You are unique. Nobody is quite like you. How amazing is that?

26 JANUARY

The days are still dark but they are getting lighter and longer all the time.

27 JANUARY

Digital detox! Have a day without social media and see how much more you get done.

28 JANUARY

Choose a stop word to use when you find yourself dwelling on critical thoughts. Any silly word will do. Say it to yourself every time you catch yourself going down that road.

29 JANUARY

Envy is natural but can be self-destructive. Use it instead as a motivational tool to inspire you to be the best version of you.

30 JANUARY

Clear out your wardrobe and give unwanted garments to a charity shop. Having more space will make you feel lighter and more organized and you will be doing someone a good turn at the same time.

31 JANUARY

January is at an end and spring is around the corner.
Make a list of all the things you are grateful for.

....

....

....

....

....

....

....

....

....

....

....

February

1 FEBRUARY

This is your journey towards empowerment and finding the courage to live the life you want, your way.

2 FEBRUARY

Do something kind for someone else. Buy a colleague a coffee, help a stranger, leave a generous tip in a restaurant, pay someone a compliment or simply smile at somebody.

3 FEBRUARY

Make a change from your routine today: walk instead of taking the bus, cook a new dish; anything that will make you feel energised and inspired.

4 FEBRUARY

Have a coffee with a friend today. Share what you both like best about each other.

---

5 FEBRUARY

Be willing to try the new and unfamiliar, however scary this may seem at first.

---

6 FEBRUARY

If someone or something makes you feel uncomfortable, listen to yourself and walk away or switch off.

7 FEBRUARY

You are: Lovable • Likeable • Intelligent • Capable •
Possessed of many talents.

Ask your friends what they think are the best things
about you, and list them here:

8 FEBRUARY

Choose a simple affirmation such as 'I love myself' and repeat it to yourself until it becomes second nature.

9 FEBRUARY

When I am having a low day, I try to dress for success.
Why not wear an accessory that makes you feel fabulous today.
A statement necklace, perhaps, or a bright lipstick?

10 FEBRUARY

If you feel scared about what's ahead, look to others
who got there before you.

11 FEBRUARY

Forgiveness is freedom. If you are nursing a grievance or
resentment against someone, then let it go.

What did you love doing as a child? It's good to remember things you used to find fun. Jot them down and try to rekindle that sense of joy you had when you were little.

13 FEBRUARY

Be kind to yourself today. Time for a bit of self-love.

14 FEBRUARY

Work on being in love with the person in the mirror who has been through so much but is still standing.

15 FEBRUARY

Have a big heart and be generous with your time today.

16 FEBRUARY

Close your eyes and imagine you are the best possible version of yourself. That's who you really are. Let go of any part of you that doesn't believe it.

17 FEBRUARY

True beauty is the human spirit, which is
fed by inner confidence.

18 FEBRUARY

Think of setbacks as obstacles you step around on
your path to success.

19 FEBRUARY

With every challenge comes fulfilment and with every
disappointment comes strength.

20 FEBRUARY

Find some balance in your life. You don't have to go for a run or to the gym every day. Some days it's fine to curl up with a book and a slice of chocolate cake.

21 FEBRUARY

Remember, you are enough.

22 FEBRUARY

Try to be accepting of your body. It is incredible what it is capable of.

23 FEBRUARY

Have faith that you will find joy and contentment
today and every day.

24 FEBRUARY

We fall in love with someone because they make us laugh,
they are caring and we find them interesting. We don't care
if they have a big nose or wobbly thighs. Be kind to yourself.

25 FEBRUARY

Try to enjoy the present moment. Often the magic is right there in front of us, as long as we take the time to notice it.

26 FEBRUARY

Open your heart to trust today; an open heart will draw others towards you.

27 FEBRUARY

Surprise someone with a random act of kindness today,
as big or as small as you like.

28 FEBRUARY

Every day is a fresh start. Put yesterday behind you and deal
with what is in front of you. Let today be positive and productive.

1 MARCH

Laughter really is the best medicine. Share your sense of humour and raise your spirits and those of everyone around you.

2 MARCH

Try to be a good listener, especially to those closest to you.

3 MARCH

Try your best today. Whatever you are doing, do it as well as you can. Your satisfaction will be your reward.

4 MARCH

We are more than how we look, and more than the things that we own. Our souls are beautiful, and we all have a part to play in this exciting world.

....

....

....

....

....

....

....

....

....

5 MARCH

Be a survivor not a victim by turning negatives into positives.

Instead of 'Why me?' think 'I can overcome this.'

6 MARCH

Put on a brave face. You've got to fake it to make it and acting confidently can work wonders.

7 MARCH

Confidence is about knowing what you want and what you deserve.

8 MARCH

Aim for progress, not perfection.

9 MARCH

Try something new today. When we do new things
we grow as people.

10 MARCH

Anger is a waste of time and serves no one.

---

11 MARCH

Do something small for yourself. Paint your nails or try a face mask. A bit of self-love is never wasted.

---

12 MARCH

It's more important to try than to succeed.

13 MARCH

Do you have any bad habits that you would like to break?
Make a note of them here.

14 MARCH

Try to work out why you have fallen into that habit.
What need does it fulfil?

15 MARCH

How could you meet that need with another,
less-destructive behaviour?

16 MARCH

Make a small adjustment that will make you happy.
For example, leave work half an hour earlier to spend time
with your child or go to that yoga class you always miss.
A minor adjustment can make a big difference.

17 MARCH

Whatever you do, give it your all. Throw yourself in with
confidence and put doubts and fears aside.

18 MARCH

Living a full and happy life involves taking risks.
Don't be scared of them, embrace them!

19 MARCH

Don't wait for life to happen – make it happen. Stepping
outside our comfort zone is part of the journey to make
our dreams come true.

20 MARCH

Opportunity doesn't always land on our doorstep. We have to be
bold to make things happen for ourselves.

21 MARCH

Be kind and generous to those around you. Studies have
shown that people who give tend to be happier and more
fulfilled than people who don't. The happier you are, the more
confident you will be.

22 MARCH

Is there a situation in your life that is making you feel
out of control? Acknowledge it here. Don't let it have any
power over you.

23 MARCH

Seek out some positive news stories today.

24 MARCH

Make time for a healthy breakfast and start the
day on a positive note.

25 MARCH

However difficult a situation might be, there is
always a way forward.

26 MARCH

Believe in yourself.

---

27 MARCH

You know you better than anyone else does.

---

28 MARCH

When something goes wrong, don't automatically blame yourself. It may be someone else's fault.

29 MARCH

If you do make a mistake, learn from it and then move on.

Do something nice to take your mind off it.

30 MARCH

You can't choose all the outcomes in life, but you can choose
the direction you want to go in.

31 MARCH

Remember that wherever you are in life, you always
have a choice. Nobody can take that away from you.
You are the director of your own drama. Only you can
decide which path to follow.

....

....

....

....

....

....

....

....

....

....

April

1 APRIL

Laughter is good for the soul. Call someone who always make you laugh or watch an episode of your favourite comedy.

2 APRIL

Declutter! Have a spring clean and a clear out.
You will feel so positive afterwards.

3 APRIL

What food makes you feel energised and good about yourself?
Make yourself a healthy meal today.

4 APRIL

Big life changes start with small tweaks. Take your first step
towards your future today.

5 APRIL

Financial security gives you confidence. Try not to obsess over
how much money you've got, instead spend the next few days
working out a plan of how much you can earn, spend and save.

6 APRIL

Put together a monthly budget by working out your incomings and outgoings. You'll end up with a clearer picture of how much money you have to play with at the end of each month and can start saving for that holiday.

7 APRIL

What is meant for you, won't pass by you.

8 APRIL

There may not be a pot of gold at the end of a rainbow, but it is a magical thing in itself.

9 APRIL

Creativity nourishes the soul: get creative
and do the things you love.

10 APRIL

Less is more, sometimes. Think about the simple things you
enjoy and don't over-complicate life.

11 APRIL

You are always stronger than you realise. Look back to a
difficult time and marvel about how you had the strength to
get through it. These are the things that make you into a
strong, confident person.

12 APRIL

Take time to stop and appreciate the beauty of nature.
There is so much to enjoy, and it's free.

13 APRIL

Listen to your inner voice. It is your closest friend during difficult
times and will help you make good decisions.

14 APRIL

Have compassion for yourself. You're not perfect,
but you're not meant to be.

15 APRIL

What we think and what we say are just as important as what we do. The words we use to express how we feel impact how we feel. If you're constantly telling yourself 'I can't' you may start to believe that's true.

Replace these negative words with positive ones instead.

16 APRIL

Embrace the struggle and let it make you stronger.
It won't last forever.

17 APRIL

Look at yourself in the mirror and give yourself a big smile.
That's the happy, positive face that makes everyone,
including you, feel great.

18 APRIL

Tune out the negative people in your life and surround
yourself with positivity.

19 APRIL

Letting go of things that have happened to you in
the past doesn't mean accepting defeat. It's part of your
decision to move on.

20 APRIL

Try lighting a scented candle and sitting peacefully
for twenty minutes in quiet contemplation.

21 APRIL

Do you eat badly when you are stressed? Try to identify the
triggers and protect yourself from them.

22 APRIL

Are you burdened by anything? Spill it out onto the page.
You can always destroy it afterwards, but writing it down will
help you get it into perspective.

....

....

....

....

....

....

....

....

....

....

....

23 APRIL

Say 'thank you' when someone is kind to you. Everybody likes to feel appreciated, and the feel-good factor will be reciprocated.

24 APRIL

Buy or pick some fresh flowers and put them in your favourite vase.

25 APRIL

Now the mornings are lighter, try getting up a few minutes earlier and make time for some stretches.

26 APRIL

Even in our darkest times we need to count our blessings.
In fact, it is more important than ever. Remind yourself of all
the great things in your life.

27 APRIL

Practice positive affirmation by repeating a phrase to
yourself on a regular basis. Make it a part of your daily routine.
How about 'I deserve to be happy' or 'I am worthy of love'.

28 APRIL

Feeling anxious and always 'on'? Try a digital detox.
Put your phone away for the day or make a policy not to
check your phone in the evenings. It's liberating!

29 APRIL

Write a letter to somebody who has been influential in your
life and tell them how they inspired you.

 APRIL

Confidence is a little seed that can grow into something bigger. Nurture it, feed it, appreciate it, give it light and love and it will flourish.

May

1 MAY

With flowers in bloom and the days getting longer, May is one of the most optimistic times of the year. Repeat the following mantra every day to keep that hopeful feeling:

'I will see the positive side of everything that happens to me. I will see each ending as a new beginning, and each challenge as an opportunity to show how capable I am.'

....

....

....

....

....

....

....

....

....

....

....

2 MAY

Let go of things you can't change. It's liberating to realise
that if there's nothing you can do about something, then it
is pointless worrying about it.

3 MAY

Move forward just one step at a time.

4 MAY

If yesterday didn't go the way you planned, try again today.

5 MAY

What piece of music do you associate with your happiest memories? Put together a playlist and listen to it whenever you need a positive boost.

6 MAY

Fear is an invisible prison; if it controls you, you'll never feel freedom.

7 MAY

By now you will have experimented with moving outside your comfort zone. Take the next few days to think about what you have done and how these new experiences have made you feel.

8 MAY

Planned change that you have made yourself helps prepare you to cope with change you didn't plan.

9 MAY

When we're inside our comfort zone we tend not to push ourselves. When we step outside it we learn to work better and achieve more.

10 MAY

Try a visualisation exercise. Take ten minutes to imagine
yourself in a happy place.

11 MAY

Make a note of words that evoke strength and success.

12 MAY

Words are powerful. Fill your thoughts with the words that make you feel strong, happy and in control.

13 MAY

When you feel self-pity pulling you down, helping others in need will give your some perspective.

14 MAY

If you need to switch off, try some mindful doodling or colouring. Just sit down with a pencil and paper and let your subconscious do the work.

15 MAY

If you feel sluggish and lacking in motivation and concentration, take some time out in the fresh air. Even a ten-minute walk around the block will make you feel better.

16 MAY

Remind yourself that you are strong, mentally, physically and spiritually.

17 MAY

Is there somebody you know who needs cheering up? Take the time to give them a call today.

18 MAY

Struggles are part of our lives; they enrich our characters,
strengthen our souls and give us the opportunity
to try another way.

19 MAY

Gardening can be balm for the soul and very creative.
If you don't have your own outside space, can you help with
a neighbour's or volunteer in a community garden?

20 MAY

It can be difficult to motivate yourself to take exercise on your
own. What about trying a Zumba class with a friend? Or spend
some time looking into the options in your area. It's easier to
keep up the habit if you enjoy it.

21 MAY

When you look in the mirror, if you think you are looking at the problem, remember you are also looking at the solution.

---

22 MAY

The point of power is always in the present moment.

23 MAY

Whatever difficulties you have faced in the past, or are facing now, remember the power of resilience. Keep your shoulders back and your head up and look at all the possibilities ahead of you.

24 MAY

Identify the strengths you have built up over the years. Remind yourself of all you have overcome and all you have learnt. The journey is a positive one.

25 MAY

List three things you've done this month that you are proud of.
It doesn't matter how small they are.

1.

2.

3.

26 MAY

Happy thoughts help create a happy, positive body.

27 MAY

Remember that you do not have to prove yourself to anyone.

28 MAY

Only you are the expert on your life, so pay close attention to your thoughts and feelings and focus on the ones that you know are right for you.

29 MAY

Wear something in your favourite colour today.

30 MAY

Have faith that you will find joy and contentment today
and every day.

31 MAY

As the sun sets on the month of May, count your blessings.

June

1 JUNE

Let June be the month that you truly develop your happiness habits; the things you do that make you feel fantastic. There are three steps that you can explore over the next three days.

---

2 JUNE

Step one: identify what makes you happy.

Jot your ideas down here:

....

....

....

....

....

3 JUNE

Step two: get your life in balance.

You might like going to the gym and also enjoy curling up
with a glass of wine. It's getting the balance right that
will make you feel happy.

---

4 JUNE

Step three: develop new habits and stick to them
for the rest of June.

Make them part of your routine, like cleaning your teeth.

5 JUNE

Can you find time to make someone else happy today?
Take time to chat to an elderly neighbour or offer to help
someone who is struggling.

6 JUNE

Stop comparing yourself to other people. You are running
your own race and no one else's.

7 JUNE

Walking is such simple, free exercise. Most phones can now
track how many steps you take in a day. Keep a note of how many
steps you have walked over the next four days and try to better it
each day. Steps walked today:

8 JUNE

Steps walked today:

9 JUNE

Steps walked today:

10 JUNE

Steps walked today:

11 JUNE

Try to think of everything as an opportunity. Sometimes even negative experiences present us with an opportunity we wouldn't have been strong enough to pursue otherwise.

12 JUNE

Remember to look at the big picture. If you have a bad day at work, will you still be worrying about it next week? How about next month or next year? Try to let go of the things that don't really matter.

13 JUNE

Find peace and balance in your life today. Give yourself time to switch off and calm your mind.

14 JUNE

Give your best every day, for we have the power to make the world a better place for all of us.

15 JUNE

Indulge yourself. Whatever it is that feels like a treat to you, do it today. It's a small but effective reminder of the positive things in life.

16 JUNE

Love the life you have, not the one you think you should have.
Make it your own.

17 JUNE

You are not alone. Enjoy the support of shared experiences.

18 JUNE

How's the walking going? Have you found a favourite route?

Take a photo and share the inspiration with friends.

19 JUNE

Face each new day with the best of intentions. Be bold, aim high and be positive in all you do.

---

20 JUNE

How are the happiness habits going?

---

21 JUNE

Look in the mirror. Instead of panicking about the bits of your body you don't like, try to admire yourself as a whole. Step back from the self-criticism and see the bigger picture.

22 JUNE

Body language is a very powerful tool. Try standing tall and looking people directly in the eyes when you talk to them. You will appear calm and confident. With practice, this will become second nature.

23 JUNE

Be kind to yourself today. Tune in to your needs and listen to your intuition.

24 JUNE

Halfway through the year, at the time of the summer solstice, feed your spiritual side by spending some time outside. Let yourself absorb the sounds, sights and smells around you and fill yourself with regenerating light and gratitude.

25 JUNE

Spend these last few days of June really honing in
on your senses. Pay attention to small details, concentrating
on one sense every day.

---

26 JUNE

Sense one: SIGHT

What can you see that fills you with wonder?

27 JUNE

Sense two: SOUND

What can you hear when you take the time to
really listen carefully?

28 JUNE

Sense three: SMELL

What smells really good today? What memories are evoked?

29 JUNE

Sense four: TOUCH

What can you feel? Close your eyes and enjoy the sensation
of your favourite textures

---

30 JUNE

Sense five: TASTE

What tastes really explode on your tongue?
Take time to savour them.

July

1 JULY

July is the month of fun, holidays and sunshine. Breaks
from routine can be unsettling. Try to maintain some balance
in your life and set aside some calm, quiet times so that you
can enjoy the busy moments.

2 JULY

Take some time to breathe. Try repeating this:

I breathe in confidence and breathe out all fear.

3 JULY

If someone asks you what you do, reply 'Whatever it takes.'

---

4 JULY

Confidence is not 'They will like me', confidence is
'I'll be fine if they don't'.

---

5 JULY

You are capable, brave and significant, even when it
feels like you're not.

6 JULY

A million 'likes' will never be enough if you don't like yourself.

7 JULY

The greatest weapon against stress is our ability to choose one thought over another.

8 JULY

Swimming, whether it's in your local pool, or the sea, a river or a lake, is a fantastically calming activity. Enjoy the feeling of weightlessness and let the water support you physically and emotionally.

9 JULY

We spend so much time working that we need to look after ourselves in the office and avoid negative co-workers. Nothing can ruin a positive day more than a colleague who always focuses on the negative.

10 JULY

The critical voice inside your head can be your worst enemy. Try writing yourself a short, motivational message that you can repeat to silence that inner critic. Here is an example:

I am brave and confident, I can handle anything that comes my way, I am self-reliant and creative, I am a problem-solver, and I love new situations.

11 JULY

Anything that costs you your peace is too expensive.
Learn to let it go.

12 JULY

In a society that profits from your self-doubt, loving yourself
is an act of rebellion.

13 JULY

To wish you were someone else is to waste the
person that you are.

14 JULY

To protect your energy:

It's okay to cancel a commitment.

It's okay not to answer that call.

It's okay to change your mind.

It's okay to want to be alone.

It's okay to take the day off.

It's okay to do nothing.

It's okay to speak up.

It's okay to let go.

15 JULY

It's your life. Don't let anyone make you feel guilty
for living it your way.

16 JULY

Be your own kind of beautiful.

17 JULY

Believe in yourself. Want a promotion at work? The first
step to getting it is to believe that you deserve it.

18 JULY

Everyone should have a calm person they can turn to when life becomes turbulent. Who is your calm person?

19 JULY

You are someone's reason to smile.

20 JULY

Wear something that makes you feel good today. Clothing has the power to change how we perceive ourselves.

21 JULY

Being happy never goes out of style.

22 JULY

Your insecurities are lies someone told you about yourself.

23 JULY

Never argue with stupid people, they will drag you down to their level and then beat you with experience. Mark Twain

24 JULY

If you can dream it, you can do it.

---

25 JULY

Failure is not the opposite of success, it's part of success.

---

26 JULY

Write down all the positive words you can think of on post-it notes and stick them where you can't miss seeing them. Include a smiley face!

27 JULY

Just remember, you can do anything you set your mind to, but it takes action, perseverance and facing your fears.

28 JULY

You are confined only by the walls you build yourself.

29 JULY

If you want to fly you must give up what weighs you down.

30 JULY

Someday your pain will become the source of your strength.
Face it. Brave it.

31 JULY

Take a minute to reflect on the past month. What positive steps have you taken towards a life of balance, calm and confidence? Jot down anything that you've found particularly inspiring or helpful this month:

....

....

....

....

....

....

....

....

....

....

1 AUGUST

Key to confidence is knowing yourself, and you cannot know yourself unless you are really honest about your strengths and weaknesses.

2 AUGUST

List your **strengths** here:

3 AUGUST

List your **weaknesses** here:

4 AUGUST

List at least one more strength:

---

5 AUGUST

Set aside some time to think carefully about what you really want
in life. Where would you like to be this time next year?

---

6 AUGUST

Consider your weaknesses. Are any of them getting in the
way of you achieving what you want from life? If so, what
could you do to address them?

7 AUGUST

What does the most successful version of you look like?
Describe it in five words.

1. ....
2. ....
3. ....
4. ....
5. ....

8 AUGUST

Let your mirror reflect your inner beauty. It's what you feel that
counts, not how you look to others.

9 AUGUST

If someone tries to get in the way of your dreams, find another way around. Trust yourself and look instead for people who are cheering you on.

10 AUGUST

We have many tools within us. For every challenge we just need to identify the necessary tool and learn how best to use it to make our life a masterpiece.

11 AUGUST

Do something every day that challenges you. It can be anything, no matter how small.

12 AUGUST

What is your challenge today?

13 AUGUST

Every small step takes you further along the path to success.

14 AUGUST

Time for some fun today. Make a plan with a friend, do something you enjoy. A film, a walk, a book or magazine?

---

15 AUGUST

The more you can bounce back from disappointment, the sweeter your success will taste.

16 AUGUST

Going places means stepping outside of your comfort zone.

17 AUGUST

What good is success if you're not healthy enough to
enjoy it? Take the time to exercise and eat balanced meals.
You are worth it.

18 AUGUST

If you cannot do great things, do little things in a great way.

19 AUGUST

It doesn't matter how slowly you go, as long as you don't stop.

20 AUGUST

When you act as if you can do something, soon enough you
will discover that you can.

21 AUGUST

The sky is not the limit. There is a whole universe beyond it.

22 AUGUST

Try living in the moment today. Kids do this without thinking about it. Enjoying the now is great for calming nerves and easing stress.

23 AUGUST

Make positive thinking a habit, something you do every day.

24 AUGUST

Let go of worries about things you cannot control. You can only be responsible for your own behaviour.

25 AUGUST

If you have a good idea, start today.

26 AUGUST

Nothing will help you find yourself more than helping others.

27 AUGUST

Face today with optimism and joy and tomorrow
will be even better.

---

28 AUGUST

Smile. And be the reason someone else smiles today.

29 AUGUST

Share the kindness that's in your soul. Even small acts of
generosity can bring joy to you and to others.

30 AUGUST

There are many voices inside our heads. Listen only
to the positive ones.

31 AUGUST

Store up those happy summer memories to keep you going through the winter months. Write them down here:

....

....

....

....

....

....

....

....

....

....

September

1 SEPTEMBER

Harness that 'back to school' feeling and remember the thrill of that new pencil case! Every day is a good day to make a fresh start.

2 SEPTEMBER

Resilience, the ability to bounce back after setbacks, is an important tool in your confidence toolbox. **Ten steps** towards strengthened resilience coming up!

3 SEPTEMBER

Step one: don't wait for problems to disappear.

Taking action will make you feel in charge and remind
you you're not helpless.

---

4 SEPTEMBER

Step two: remind yourself of your strengths
and accomplishments.

Take a moment to think about all that you've done and
all that you are: strong, determined and capable.

5 SEPTEMBER

Step three: turn to your friends.

We need our friends in times of stress, so it is important to nurture and cherish friendships. Having someone to talk to won't make the problem go away, but it will give you comfort and support (and someone else's perspective on the problem).

6 SEPTEMBER

Step four: be flexible.

The more flexible and adaptable you are, the better you will cope with challenging times. If you are too rigid you will find it harder to take things in your stride.

7 SEPTEMBER

Step five: look after yourself.

You'll cope better in a crisis if you get enough sleep, eat well and exercise regularly.

8 SEPTEMBER

Step six: remember to think of the future.

You can't stop stressful things happening, but you can remember that, however tough the present moment is, things may feel very different in the future.

9 SEPTEMBER

Step seven: accept change.

Things are always going to change, for better and for worse,
so don't fight it. Change can feel hard, but that's normal.
A new home feels strange until it becomes familiar.

10 SEPTEMBER

Step eight: keep busy.

In a crisis, doing something is better than doing nothing.
Not only because that way things get done, but also because
when your hands are busy your mind becomes more calm.
If nothing else, put the kettle on!

11 SEPTEMBER

Step nine: do it now!

Deal with issues and challenges as they come along – don't
be the type of person who puts things off. If you're used to
being the type of person who makes that difficult call now
and not in three days' time, then you'll be much better
equipped to cope in a crisis.

12 SEPTEMBER

Step ten: be an optimist.

This isn't easy if it doesn't come naturally to you, but it's worth
trying to look at the glass-half-full, bright side of life. It will really
help you in difficult times.

13 SEPTEMBER

Don't let anything break you.

14 SEPTEMBER

Start right now. Do you want to make a positive change in your life? Do it today.

15 SEPTEMBER

Remember, in general, the world is a good place. Look for the positives and you'll find more good things will come your way.

16 SEPTEMBER

Never, ever let go of **hope**.

17 SEPTEMBER

We can't choose our differences, or those of the people we love. We can only accept them and learn to love them.

18 SEPTEMBER

Acceptance is about being realistic and practical.
It's not a weakness, it's a strength.

19 SEPTEMBER

Appreciate your happy moments and all the good things in your
life. Gratitude has so many benefits. Think about this over the
next few days ...

20 SEPTEMBER

Benefit one: gratitude increases our sense of wellbeing,
satisfaction and happiness.

21 SEPTEMBER

Benefit two: it increases our energy.

---

22 SEPTEMBER

Benefit three: it makes us more optimistic.

---

23 SEPTEMBER

Benefit four: it improves our ability to empathise with others

24 SEPTEMBER

Benefit five: it helps us sleep better.

25 SEPTEMBER

Benefit six: it makes us kinder and more compassionate.

26 SEPTEMBER

Benefit seven: it enhances the immune system.

27 SEPTEMBER

Benefit eight: it calms aggressive and angry feelings.

---

28 SEPTEMBER

If your cup is half empty, take it to the tap yourself!

---

29 SEPTEMBER

If you are facing some difficulty that seems insurmountable,
break it down into small, manageable tasks.

30 SEPTEMBER

Hopefully you are feeling **positive** and **optimistic** as summer is turning into autumn. What are you looking forward to about the coming season?

....

....

....

....

....

....

....

....

....

....

October

1 OCTOBER

The beautiful autumnal colours that October brings can lift the spirits. But it is also a month of change, as the leaves turn from green to russet and then fall from the trees. Use this month to embrace change in your life. Give some thought to tiny life adjustments you would like to introduce. Nothing big – it is the little changes that, together, contribute to significant and positive change.

To start with, think of three small changes over the next three days.

2 OCTOBER

Change one:

3 OCTOBER

Change two:

4 OCTOBER

Change three:

5 OCTOBER

How might you take steps towards these changes?

---

6 OCTOBER

Believe you can change and you'll start to see little ways you can.

---

7 OCTOBER

It's also okay to stand still and reflect sometimes,
and look back on your progress.

8 OCTOBER

Close your eyes and picture how far you have come
on your path to confidence.

9 OCTOBER

Think about your friends and family. Who amongst them has
successfully made a significant change in their life that has
contributed to their happiness and confidence?

10 OCTOBER

Whoever it is, talk to them and get them to share their story.
You will find you gain insight and inspiration.

11 OCTOBER

Stay away from negative people. They have a problem for every solution.

the

12 OCTOBER

Sometimes it's difficult to get started because we don't know where to start. Instead of looking for the start line, just begin from exactly where you are now; you'll soon be on your way.

13 OCTOBER

It's about progress not perfection.

14 OCTOBER

Try to channel excess energies into rejuvenation.

---

15 OCTOBER

Always over-deliver and under-promise.

---

16 OCTOBER

Do not give up; the beginning is always the most difficult.

17 OCTOBER

Filter your self-image. We're constantly filtering and editing our online personas – apply those same skills to your self-image. We all have a mental picture of ourselves and it determines how confident we are in ourselves.

18 OCTOBER

The past is in your head. The future is in your hands.

19 OCTOBER

Take the time to speak slowly. It is a small thing, but it
shows confidence and acknowledges that your thoughts
are worth listening to.

20 OCTOBER

You're growing in confidence every single day.
Be proud of yourself.

21 OCTOBER

There are some events we have no power over, but we do have
power over the way we react towards them.

23 OCTOBER

You can sit around waiting for life to happen, or you can
seize this very moment and make things happen.

24 OCTOBER

Remember those changes you thought about at the
start of the month? How are they going?

25 OCTOBER

Act like a kid today and shuffle through the fallen leaves.
Nothing lifts your mood like embracing playfulness!

26 OCTOBER

You have the right to choose your own path. Remember
every day that the world is full of opportunity to make your
life what you want it to be.

27 OCTOBER

The clocks are about to change and it is getting darker earlier. Think about how you can make the most of these cosy, candlelit evenings.

28 OCTOBER

Be thankful that your life isn't boring! If nothing good nor bad ever happened to you, you'd start to feel pretty bored with life.

29 OCTOBER

Time to get out your favourite, cosiest winter jumpers.

30 OCTOBER

If you take care of today, tomorrow will take care of itself.

31 OCTOBER

Thank you, October, for giving me the opportunity to make these positive changes in my life:

....

....

....

....

....

....

....

....

....

....

....

November

1 NOVEMBER

November is a good month for rekindling friendships
and for sharing good food and laughter.

2 NOVEMBER

Reconnect with people you haven't seen for a while.

Get those diaries out and make a plan to meet. It doesn't matter
if it's way in the future. The date will soon come around and
you'll have even more to catch up on.

3 NOVEMBER

Is it time for a new winter hairstyle? Even a fringe trim
will give you a boost!

4 NOVEMBER

Wear a bright colour today and make yourself smile.

5 NOVEMBER

What's stopping you? When you are facing some difficulty that seems insurmountable, write down a list of thoughts that are stopping you from dealing with it. They are likely to be something like this:

- This is too hard.
- I'm bound to fail.
- Maybe I should try to forget about it for now.
- It's too much for me.
- What's the point anyway?

Now write your own list and over the next few days, see if you can find an alternative thought for each one.

Your list:

....

....

....

....

....

....

....

6 NOVEMBER

Alternative thought (example): this is very hard, but I need to remember that I have come through tough times before and therefore I can do so again.

Add your own alternative thought here:

7 NOVEMBER

Alternative thought (example): I do fear failure, but I am not the sort of person who gives up easily and today I'm going to think of two things that might help me start dealing with this problem.

Your own alternative thought:

8 NOVEMBER

Alternative thought:

9 NOVEMBER

Alternative thought:

10 NOVEMBER

Alternative thought:

11 NOVEMBER

Once you get your mind into problem-solving mode, you'll be amazed how much you can achieve.

12 NOVEMBER

Perhaps you can help a friend do the same, and then encourage each other in your alternative thinking?

13 NOVEMBER

The way you choose to interpret events is powerful, so why not choose to interpret them in a way that recognises your strengths and allows you to move forward feeling good about yourself?

14 NOVEMBER

Everybody feels anxious from time to time. It's quite natural and does have a positive side, in that it can drive us to get things done. But high levels of anxiety often go hand-in-hand with low self-esteem and lack of confidence.

The good news is that there is a lot you can do to combat anxiety.

15 NOVEMBER

Start by noticing what makes you anxious. This is the key to unlocking the chains of anxiety.

Some common causes are listed on the following days. Take the time to jot down what you think your personal causes of anxiety are too.

16 NOVEMBER

Are you online a lot? Checking social media and reading about other people's lives may be causing you to feel anxious about your own life. Try a digital detox.

17 NOVEMBER

Are you thinking about work problems or goals? Try to switch off at the end of the day. You are more than just a colleague.

18 NOVEMBER

Are you still going over and over past events? Let go of the past by looking at the bigger picture and actively taking your thoughts in another direction.

19 NOVEMBER

Do you feel fearful about the future? Work on your visualisation. Picture where you would like to see yourself in the future and then start to plot out how you might get there.

---

20 NOVEMBER

Do you constantly find fault with the way you do things throughout the day? Stop letting negative thoughts control you.

---

21 NOVEMBER

The key is not to ignore what is making you anxious, but by identifying the cause you can work towards changing the effects.

22 NOVEMBER

Deep breathing is the doorway to a world of peace and relaxation. Find somewhere comfortable and start by breathing consciously and slowly. Become aware of its sound and flow and try not to think of anything else. You could repeat the word 'calm' as you inhale and 'relax' as you exhale.

Doing this will seem like a challenge at first but if you practise it regularly it will become easier. Set aside five or ten minutes every day over the next week and see if it can become one of your happiness habits.

23 NOVEMBER

How's the exercise regime going? You might have had to make some changes because of the shorter days. Perhaps now is a good time to try that yoga class?

24 NOVEMBER

Or perhaps try a meditation class? You could team up with a friend.

25 NOVEMBER

Laughter is a great anxiety-buster. Seek out a friend
who always makes you laugh.

26 NOVEMBER

Real confidence is a state of mind that you can choose or learn to
develop and use for yourself in all areas of your life.

27 NOVEMBER

Does the change of season affect how you are feeling?

If the darker evenings make you feel blue, try to get outside in the middle of the day as much as you can. Even a brisk walk around the block can make you feel much brighter.

28 NOVEMBER

New experiences and broader horizons will make you more creative.

29 NOVEMBER

Don't block your own path. The blocks that you place on yourself can only hold you back in life.

....

....

....

....

....

....

....

....

....

....

30 NOVEMBER

To end the month, try a visualisation exercise. Instead of feeling fearful, focus your mind on the end result and visualise yourself in that relationship, working in your dream job, living your dream life. This will help you shift a gear in your mind, moving your life forward and away from fearful thoughts.

December

1 DECEMBER

The crazy **party season** is almost upon us. Take care to
carve out some down-time this month.

2 DECEMBER

Before you start your Christmas shopping, have a careful thought
about what people would like. The most welcome gift is not
usually the one that cost the earth. Get crafty and make
some of your presents this year.

3 DECEMBER

Christmas is a tough time for some people, whether due
to bereavement or a difficult personal situation, or just plain
loneliness. If you know anyone this applies to, contact them
and let them know you are there for them.

4 DECEMBER

Look after yourself and make sure you get your five a day.

5 DECEMBER

Look back on all that you have achieved this year. You have worked hard and have come a long way. You deserve to give yourself a pat on the back.

6 DECEMBER

When you remember to focus on other people's good qualities, you will be reminded there is good in everyone.

7 DECEMBER

Reinforce the actions that do you good and stop those
that do you harm – both mentally and physically – before
they become a habit.

8 DECEMBER

Sometimes you don't know how well you can cope until you
are tested. When things get difficult you can find your strength
emerges and you discover how big you are.

9 DECEMBER

Get into the Christmas spirit and do some festive baking.
Gingerbread and spicy fruit cakes will fill your home
with happy smells.

10 DECEMBER

Forgive yourself for any mistakes you feel you've made in the
past. Only once you've forgiven yourself, can you really move on.

11 DECEMBER

Make a list of all the people you would like to thank
for their friendship this year.

12 DECEMBER

Why not send each of them a Christmas card?
You know they'll appreciate it.

13 DECEMBER

Do something you've been procrastinating about.
We all have things on our to-do lists that have
been sitting there for ages. Tick it off before
the end of the year.

14 DECEMBER

Give yourself time to relax today. Pace yourself and you will
have more energy to really enjoy the Christmas break.

15 DECEMBER

When things feel out of control, recall moments when you felt
safe – today you can live them and breathe them again and
cherish the peaceful spirit these memories bring.

16 DECEMBER

Practise some gratitude today. Who has supported you in your confidence journey this year? Let them know how much you appreciate them being there for you.

17 DECEMBER

Shine your positive energy and self-belief on others and it will be reflected back at you.

18 DECEMBER

Clear your desk. It might seem like a small thing but it is a way of regaining control.

19 DECEMBER

Put on some Christmas music and get some of that gift-wrapping done.

20 DECEMBER

Smile! Even if you're not feeling it, smile – it'll make you feel better.

21 DECEMBER

Try something new today. Discover a new podcast, take a different route or browse through your local library or bookshop for a new author.

22 DECEMBER

Remind yourself of how far you've come in your journey; what you confidently do today you may have feared to attempt last week, month or year.

23 DECEMBER

Once you decide what you truly want in life, you can go
out and make it happen.

24 DECEMBER

Kiss someone under the mistletoe!

25 DECEMBER

Receiving brings fleeting happiness but giving makes the feeling last. What are the things that made you happy today? Write them down so that you can reflect on them later:

....

....

....

....

....

....

....

....

....

20 DECEMBER

Time spent with those you love is never time wasted.

27 DECEMBER

Don't feel guilty about the lapse in your diet and exercise regime,
just enjoy spending the time with your friends and family.

28 DECEMBER

Patience and kindness and tolerance are essential qualities that we should all cultivate. If someone or something irritates you, breathe deeply and count to ten. The moment will pass and you will be grateful that you kept calm.

29 DECEMBER

Get active. Doing something is always better than not doing anything.

30 DECEMBER

We are all capable of extraordinary things; the spirit is within us
to march forward even when the road seems full of obstacles.

31 DECEMBER

We cannot know the future, but we can plan for it. But before you do that, take some time to reflect on all you have discovered and achieved over the past year.

You are amazing and will continue to go from strength to strength.

What has been the highlight of your year? Record it here:

....

....

....

....

....

....

....

....

....

....

NEW YEAR,

NEW CONFIDENT

YOU!!

IN THE LAST YEAR I HAVE ACHIEVED ALL THIS:

....

....

....

....

....

....

....

....

....

....

....

....

NEW YEAR'S RESOLUTIONS:

....

....

....

....

....

....

....

....

....

....

....

....

NOTES

NOTES

NOTES

NOTES

NOTES

NOTES

ALSO BY KATIE PIPER:

Beautiful

Things Get Better

Start Your Day with Katie

Beautiful Ever After

Confidence

From Mother to Daughter